Portuguese Dialogues for Beginners
Book 2

Over 100 Daily Used Phrases and Short Stories to Learn Portuguese in Your Car. Have Fun and Grow Your Vocabulary with Crazy Effective Language Learning Lessons

www.LearnLikeNatives.com

www.LearnLikeNatives.com

© Copyright 2020
By Learn Like A Native

ALL RIGHTS RESERVED

No part of this book may be reproduced, stored in a retrieval system, or transmitted in any form or by any means, without the prior written permission of the publisher.

www.LearnLikeNatives.com

TABLE OF CONTENT

INTRODUCTION	5
CHAPTER 1 John's Homework /	
School + Classroom	17
Translation of the Story	17
John's Homework	33
CHAPTER 2 Thrift Store Bargain /	
house and furniture	41
Translation of the Story	41
Thrift Store Bargain	55
CHAPTER 3 The Goat /	
common present tense verbs	63
Translation of the Story	79
The Goat	79
CONCLUSION	89
About the Author	95

www.LearnLikeNatives.com

www.LearnLikeNatives.com

INTRODUCTION

Before we dive into some Brazilian Portuguese, I want to congratulate you, whether you're just beginning, continuing, or resuming your language learning journey. Here at Learn Like a Native, we understand the determination it takes to pick up a new language and after reading this book, you'll be another step closer to achieving your language goals.

As a thank you for learning with us, we are giving you free access to our 'Speak Like a Native' eBook. It's packed full of practical advice and insider tips on how to make language learning quick, easy, and most importantly, enjoyable. Head over to LearnLikeNatives.com to access your free guide and peruse our huge selection of language learning resources.

Learning a new language is a bit like cooking—you need several different ingredients and the right technique, but the end result is sure to be delicious. We created this book of short stories for learning Brazilian Portuguese because language is alive. Language is about the senses—hearing, tasting the words on your tongue, and touching another culture up close. Learning a language in a classroom is a fine place to start, but it's not a complete introduction to a language.

In this book, you'll find a language come to life. These short stories are miniature immersions into the Brazilian Portuguese language, at a level that is perfect for beginners. This book is not a lecture on grammar. It's not an endless vocabulary list. This book is the closest you can come to a language immersion without leaving the country. In the stories within, you will see people speaking to each other, going through daily life situations, and using the most common, helpful words and phrases in language. You are holding the key to bringing your Brazilian Portuguese studies to life.

Made for Beginners

We made this book with beginners in mind. You'll find that the language is simple, but not boring. Most of the book is in the present tense, so you will be able to focus on dialogues, root verbs, and understand and find patterns in subject-verb agreement.

This is not "just" a translated book. While reading novels and short stories translated into Brazilian Portuguese is a wonderful thing, beginners (and even novices) often run into difficulty. Literary licenses and complex sentence structure can make reading in your second language truly difficult—

not to mention BORING. That's why Brazilian Portuguese Short Stories for Beginners is the perfect book to pick up. The stories are simple, but not infantile. They were not written for children, but the language is simple so that beginners can pick it up.

The Benefits of Learning a Second Language

If you have picked up this book, it's likely that you are already aware of the many benefits of learning a second language. Besides just being fun, knowing more than one language opens up a whole new world to you. You will be able to communicate with a much larger chunk of the world. Opportunities in the workforce will open up, and maybe even your day-to-day work will be improved. Improved communication can also help you expand your business. And from a

www.LearnLikeNatives.com

neurological perspective, learning a second language is like taking your daily vitamins and eating well, for your brain!

How To Use The Book

The chapters of this book all follow the same structure:

- A short story with several dialogs
- A summary in Brazilian Portuguese
- A list of important words and phrases and their English translation
- Questions to test your understanding
- Answers to check if you were right
- The English translation of the story to clear every doubt

www.LearnLikeNatives.com

You may use this book however is comfortable for you, but we have a few recommendations for getting the most out of the experience. Try these tips and if they work for you, you can use them on every chapter throughout the book.

1) Start by reading the story all the way through. Don't stop or get hung up on any particular words or phrases. See how much of the plot you can understand in this way. We think you'll get a lot more of it than you may expect, but it is completely normal not to understand everything in the story. You are learning a new language, and that takes time.

2) Read the summary in Brazilian Portuguese. See if it matches what you have understood of the plot.

3) Read the story through again, slower this time. See if you can pick up the meaning of any words or phrases you don't understand by using context clues and the information from the summary.

4) Test yourself! Try to answer the five comprehension questions that come at the end of each story. Write your answers down, and then check them against the answer key. How did you do? If you didn't get them all, no worries!

5) Look over the vocabulary list that accompanies the chapter. Are any of these the words you did not understand? Did you already know the meaning of some of them from your reading?

6) Now go through the story once more. Pay attention this time to the words and phrases you haven't understand. If you'd like, take the time to look them up to

expand your meaning of the story. Every time you read over the story, you'll understand more and more.

7) Move on to the next chapter when you are ready.

Read and Listen

The audio version is the best way to experience this book, as you will hear a native Brazilian Portuguese speaker tell you each story. You will become accustomed to their accent as you listen along, a huge plus for when you want to apply your new language skills in the real world.

If this has ignited your language learning passion and you are keen to find out what other resources are available, go to LearnLikeNatives.com,

www.LearnLikeNatives.com

where you can access our vast range of free learning materials. Don't know where to begin? An excellent place to start is our 'Speak Like a Native' free eBook, full of practical advice and insider tips on how to make language learning quick, easy, and most importantly, enjoyable.

And remember, small steps add up to great advancements! No moment is better to begin learning than the present.

www.LearnLikeNatives.com

FREE BOOK!

Get the *FREE BOOK* that reveals the secrets path to learn any language fast, and without leaving your country.

Discover:

- The **language 5 golden rules** to master languages at will

- Proven **mind training techniques** to revolutionize your learning

- A complete step-by-step guide to **conquering any language**

www.LearnLikeNatives.com

www.LearnLikeNatives.com

www.LearnLikeNatives.com

CHAPTER 1
John's Homework / School + Classroom

HISTÓRIA

A Sra. Kloss é **professora** da 4ª série. Ela dá aulas na Homewood Elementary School. A **escola** fica em um prédio de tijolos vermelhos. Ela fica em uma cidade pequena.

A Sra. Kloss tem uma **turma** de 15 alunos. Seus **alunos** são meninos e meninas. Eles geralmente são bons alunos. A Sra. Kloss tem uma rotina. Os alunos começam o dia em suas **mesas**, sentados em suas **cadeiras**. Sra. Kloss faz a **chamada**.

— Louise? — ela diz.

— Aqui! — grita Louise.

— Mike? — diz a Sra. Kloss.

— Presente — diz Mike.

— João?

— Aqui, Sra. Kloss— diz João.

E assim por diante. Após a chamada, a Sra. Kloss começa o dia com **matemática**. Para seus alunos, matemática é difícil. A turma escuta as explicações da Sra. Kloss. Eles leem o que ela escreve no **quadro-negro**. Às vezes, um aluno resolve um problema na frente da turma. Eles usam **giz** para escrever a solução. Os outros alunos fazem os problemas em seus **cadernos**.

A hora favorita de todos é o almoço. A turma vai para o refeitório. Eles têm duas opções. Uma opção é uma refeição saudável, com carne e legumes. A outra opção é pizza ou hambúrguer. Alguns alunos trazem o almoço de casa.

À tarde, eles estudam **história**. Nas sextas-feiras, eles têm aula de **ciências** no **laboratório**. Eles fazem **experimentos**, como cultivar plantas em um pedaço de batata.

A Sra. Kloss passa **lição de casa** para seus alunos todos os dias. Eles levam o trabalho para casa. Eles fazem a lição à noite. No dia seguinte, trazem para a escola. A única desculpa para lições de casa incompletas é um bilhete dos pais.

Um dia, a turma revisa junta a lição de casa de **inglês**.

— Todos, por favor, ponham os **trabalhos** na minha mesa — diz a Sra. Kloss. Todos entregam a lição de casa para a Sra. Kloss. Todos, exceto o João.

— João, onde está sua lição de casa? — diz a Sra. Kloss.

O rosto do João está muito vermelho. Ele está nervoso.

— Eu não trouxe — diz João.

— Você tem um bilhete dos seus pais? — pergunta a Sra. Kloss.

— Não — diz João.

— Então por que você não fez sua lição de casa? — pergunta Sra. Kloss. João diz algo em voz muito baixa.

— O quê? Não conseguimos escutar — diz a Sra. Kloss. Ela dá um sorriso simpático para o João. Ele parece nervoso.

— Meu cachorro comeu minha lição de casa — diz João. A Sra. Kloss e os outros alunos riem. Essa é a desculpa mais comum de quem não faz a lição.

— Está na sua **mochila**? Ou talvez no seu **armário**? — pergunta a Sra. Kloss. Ela quer ajudar o João.

— Não, meu cachorro comeu! — insiste João.

— Essa é a **desculpa mais velha do mundo** — diz a Sra. Kloss.

— É verdade! — diz João. João é um bom aluno. Ele geralmente tira **nota A em tudo**. A Sra. Kloss não quer mandar o João para a **sala do diretor** por mentir. Ela não acredita no João, mas decide lhe dar outra chance.

— Traga a lição de casa amanhã — diz a Sra. Kloss. — Aqui está outra cópia. — João pega a **folha de exercícios** e agradece à Sra. Kloss. A turma pega seus cadernos de **artes**. Na aula de artes de hoje, eles estão desenhando um quadro com **lápis** de cor. Os alunos adoram a aula de artes. É uma chance de relaxar. Eles desenham e desenham até a **sineta** tocar. O dia de aula acabou.

Os alunos conversam nos corredores. Eles trocam anotações. Os alunos da 4ª série esperam do lado de fora. Seus pais os buscam. Alguns deles estão a pé. Alguns estão de carro. Os professores lhes ajudam a encontrar seus pais.

A Sra. Kloss termina seu trabalho. Ela guarda seu **laptop** na bolsa. Sua sala de aula está limpa e vazia. Ela sai da escola. Enquanto ela caminha até o carro, ela vê João e seu pai. O pai de João vem buscá-lo com o cachorro. A Sra. Kloss acena para João e seu pai.

— Olá, João! — diz a Sra. Kloss.

— Boa tarde, Sra. Kloss — diz João.

— É este o cachorro que comeu sua lição de casa? — pergunta a Sra. Kloss. Ela sorri, então João sabe que ela está brincando.

— Sim, Sra. Kloss — diz o pai do João. — Obrigada por entender. O João está com tanto medo de se meter em problemas!

A Sra. Kloss está chocada! Desta vez, o cachorro realmente comeu a lição de casa.

www.LearnLikeNatives.com

LISTA DE VOCABULÁRIO

Teacher	Professor
School	Escola
Class	Turma
Students	Alunos
Desk	Mesa
Chair	Cadeira
Roll call	Chamada
Math	Matemática
Blackboard	Quadro-negro
Chalk	Giz
Notebook	Caderno

www.LearnLikeNatives.com

History	História
Science	Ciências
Lab	Laboratório
Experiment	Experimento
Homework	Lição de casa
English	Inglês
Papers	Trabalhos
Backpack	Mochila
Locker	Armário
The oldest excuse in the book	A desculpa mais velha do mundo
Straight a's	Nota a em tudo
Principal's office	Sala do diretor
Worksheet	Folha de exercícios

www.LearnLikeNatives.com

Pencils	Lápis
Bell	Sineta
Laptop	Laptop

PERGUNTAS

1) Como começa o dia na sala de aula da Sra. Kloss?

    a) os alunos se levantam e gritam

    b) com uma lição de casa

    c) com a chamada

    d) a Sra. Kloss grita

2) Qual é a hora do dia favorita de todos na Homewood Elementary School?

    a) chamada

    b) hora do almoço

    c) aula de matemática

    d) depois da sineta tocar

3) Por que a Sra. Kloss diz que a desculpa de João é a mais velha do mundo?

    a) porque todos usam essa desculpa

    b) João é o mais velho da turma

    c) ele esqueceu seu livro

    d) seu cachorro tem sete anos

4) O que você precisa ter se não fizer a lição de casa?

    a) um experimento científico

    b) uma boa desculpa

    c) nada, está tudo bem

    d) um bilhete dos seus pais

5) Por que a Sra. Kloss está surpresa no final da história?

a) ela percebe que João estava dizendo a verdade

b) o cachorro do João na verdade é um cavalo

c) o João não fala com ela

d) o pai do João se parece muito com ele

www.LearnLikeNatives.com

RESPOSTAS

1) Como começa o dia na sala de aula da Sra. Kloss?

    c) com a chamada

2) Qual é a hora do dia favorita de todos na Homewood Elementary School?

    b) hora do almoço

3) Por que a Sra. Kloss diz que a desculpa do João é a mais velha do mundo?

    a) porque todos usam essa desculpa

4) O que você precisa ter se não fizer a lição de casa?

    d) um bilhete dos seus pais

www.LearnLikeNatives.com

5) Por que a Sra. Kloss está surpresa no final da história?

a) ela percebe que o João estava dizendo a verdade

www.LearnLikeNatives.com

Translation of the Story

John's Homework

STORY

Mrs. Kloss is a grade 4 **teacher**. She teaches at Homewood Elementary School. The **school** is in a red brick building. It is in a small town.

Mrs. Kloss has a **class** of 15 students. Her **students** are boys and girls. They are usually good students. Mrs. Kloss has a routine. Her students start the day at their **desks**, seated in their **chairs**. Mrs. Kloss calls **roll call**.

"Louise?" she says.

"Here!" shouts Louise.

"Mike?" says Mrs. Kloss.

"Present," says Mike.

"John?"

"Here, Mrs. Kloss," John says.

And so on. After roll call, Mrs. Kloss starts the day with **math**. For her students, math is difficult. The class listens to Mrs. Kloss teach. They watch as she writes on the **blackboard**. Sometimes, one student solves a problem in front of the class. They use **chalk** to write out the solution. The other students do the problems in their **notebooks**.

Everyone's favorite time is lunch time. The class goes to the lunchroom. They have two choices. One choice is a healthy meal of meat and vegetables. The other choice is pizza or hamburgers. Some students bring a lunch from home.

In the afternoon, they study **history**. On Fridays, they have **science** class in the **lab**. They do **experiments**, like growing plants from a piece of potato.

Mrs. Kloss gives her students **homework** every day. They take the work home. They work at night. The next day, they bring it to school. The only excuse for incomplete homework is a note from their parents.

One day, the class reviews the **English** homework together.

"Everyone, please bring your **papers** to my desk," says Mrs. Kloss. Everyone brings their homework to Mrs. Kloss. Everyone except for John.

"John, where is your homework?" says Mrs. Kloss.

John's face is very red. He is nervous.

"I don't have it," says John.

"Do you have a note from your parents?" asks Mrs. Kloss.

"No," says John.

"Why didn't you do your homework, then?" asks Mrs. Kloss. John says something very quietly.

"What? We can't hear you," says Mrs. Kloss. She gives John a kind smile. He looks nervous.

"My dog ate my homework," says John. Mrs. Kloss and the other students laugh. This excuse is the most typical excuse for not having work done.

"Is it in your **backpack**? Or maybe your **locker**?" asks Mrs. Kloss. She wants to help John.

"No, my dog ate it!" insists John.

"That's the **oldest excuse in the book**," says Mrs. Kloss.

"It is true!" says John. John is a good student. He usually makes **straight A's**. Mrs. Kloss does not want to send Jon to the **principal's office** for lying. She does not believe John, but she decides to give him another chance.

"Bring the homework tomorrow," says Mrs. Kloss. "Here is another copy." John takes the **worksheet** and thanks Mrs. Kloss. The class turns to their **art** notebook. Today in art class they are drawing a picture with colored **pencils**. Students love art class. It is a chance to relax. They draw and draw until the **bell** rings. School is over.

Students talk in the hallways. They exchange notes. The Grade 4 students wait outside. Their parents pick them up. Some of them are on foot. Some of them are in cars. The teachers help them to find their parents.

Mrs. Kloss finishes her work. She packs her **laptop** into her bag. Her classroom is clean and empty. She goes outside. As she walks to her car, she see John and his dad. John's father picks him up with their dog. Mrs. Kloss waves to John and his father.

"Hello, John!" says Mrs. Kloss.

"Good afternoon, Mrs. Kloss," John says.

"Is this the dog that ate your homework?" asks Mrs. Kloss. She smiles, so John knows she is teasing.

"Yes, Mrs. Kloss," says John's father. "Thank you for understanding. John is so worried about getting in trouble!"

Mrs. Kloss is shocked! This time, the dog really did eat the homework.

www.LearnLikeNatives.com

CHAPTER 2
Thrift Store Bargain / house and furniture

HISTÓRIA

Louise e Mary são melhores amigas. Elas também **moram juntas**. Elas dividem um **apartamento** no centro da cidade. Hoje elas querem comprar **móveis** para seu **lar**. Louise e Mary são estudantes. Elas não têm muito dinheiro.

— Onde podemos fazer compras? — Louise pergunta a Mary.

— Precisamos de muitos móveis — diz Mary. Ela está preocupada com o dinheiro.

— Eu sei — diz Louise. — Precisamos encontrar uma **pechincha**.

— Tenho uma ideia. Vamos ao brechó! — diz Mary.

— Boa ideia! — diz Louise.

As duas meninas vão de carro para o brechó. É uma loja gigante. O prédio é maior que dez **casas**.

As meninas estacionam o carro. O estacionamento está vazio.

— Uau — diz Louise. — A loja é muito grande.

— Totalmente — diz Mary. — E não tem ninguém aqui.

— Seremos as únicas pessoas — diz Louise. — Podemos **ficar à vontade**.

As meninas entram na loja. A loja tem de tudo. À direita fica a seção de **cozinha**. Há **refrigeradores** altos e **micro-ondas** antigos nas **prateleiras**. Há **torradeiras** de todas as cores. Os preços são bons. Um micro-ondas custa apenas $10.

Tudo é uma pechincha. Os itens são usados e de segunda mão. No entanto, Mary e Louise encontram coisas de que elas gostam. Há mais de uma dúzia de sofás. Mary e Louise precisam de um **sofá**. Elas ficam um tempo falando sobre os diferentes sofás. Mary gosta de um sofá de couro marrom. Louise gosta de um grande sofá roxo. Elas não conseguem decidir. Louise vê uma **cadeira** roxa. As meninas decidem comprar a cadeira e o sofá roxos para combinar. É perfeito para a casa delas.

— Preciso de uma **cama** para o meu **quarto** — diz Louise.

As meninas vão para a área dos quartos. Primeiro, passam pela seção de arte.

— Sabe, precisamos de algo para as **paredes** — diz Louise. Mary concorda. Há grandes pinturas, pequenas pinturas, **molduras** vazias e fotografias emolduradas. Louise escolhe uma grande pintura abstrata. Ela tem linhas salpicadas de tinta vermelha, azul e preta.

— Eu posso pintar desse jeito — diz Mary. — Parece uma pintura de criança.

— É só $5 — diz Louise.

— Ah, ok! — diz Mary.

www.LearnLikeNatives.com

As meninas terminam as compras. Louise também encontra uma **luminária** para o seu quarto. O quarto dela é muito escuro. Mary escolhe um tapete para o banheiro. As meninas estão muito felizes. Elas gastam apenas $100 dólares em todos os móveis.

— É por isso que comprar no brechó é uma pechincha — diz Louise.

— Sim, compramos **tudo e mais alguma coisa**! — diz Mary.

Mary e Louise fazem uma festa em seu apartamento naquela noite. É uma festa para receber os amigos. Mary e Louise querem mostrar seus móveis novos.

A campainha toca. Mary abre a **porta**. O Nick é o primeiro a chegar. O Nick é amigo da Mary. O Nick também é estudante. Ele estuda história da arte.

— Oi, senhoras — diz Nick. — Obrigado por me convidarem.

— Entre, Nick! — diz Mary. Nick entra no **hall de entrada**. Ela o abraça.

— Quer ver nossas coisas novas? — pergunta Louise.

— Sim! — diz Nick.

Louise e Mary mostram o apartamento para Nick. Elas estão felizes com a **sala de estar**. A cadeira, o quadro e o sofá novos estão muito bonitos.

— Tudo isso é do brechó — diz Mary. Ela está orgulhosa.

Nick vai até o quadro. — Gosto muito desta pintura — diz ele.

— Eu também — diz Louise. — Eu que escolhi.

— Me lembra o Jackson Pollock — diz Nick.

— Quem é Jackson Pollock? — pergunta Mary.

— Ele é um pintor muito famoso — diz Nick. — Ele salpica tinta na tela. Assim como neste quadro. — Nick olha atentamente para a pintura.

— É assinada? — ele pergunta. Louise faz que não com a cabeça. — Vamos ver o lado de trás, então.

Eles tiram a pintura da moldura e a viram. Todos estão em silêncio. Na parte inferior, há uma assinatura que se parece com "Jackson Pollock".

— Quanto você pagou por isso? — pergunta Nick.

— Uns $5 — diz Louise.

— Esse quadro provavelmente vale pelo menos $10 milhões de dólares — diz Nick. Ele está chocado. Mary olha para Louise. Louise olha para Mary.

— Alguém quer uma taça de champanhe? — diz Mary.

Isso é que é uma pechincha!

www.LearnLikeNatives.com

LISTA DE VOCABULÁRIO

Roommates	Morar junto
Apartment	Apartamento
Furniture	Móveis
Home	Lar
Bargain	Pechincha
Thrift store	Brechó
House	Casa
Make ourselves at home	Ficar à vontade
Kitchen	Cozinha
Refrigerators	Refrigeradores
Microwaves	Micro-ondas

Shelves	Prateleiras
Toasters	Torradeiras
Chair	Cadeira
Table	Mesa
Sofa	Sofá
Bed	Cama
Bedroom	Quarto
Wall	Parede
Frame	Moldura
Lamp	Luminária
Carpet	Tapete
Bathroom	Banheiro
Everything but the kitchen sink	Tudo e mais um pouco

Door	Porta
Foyer	Hall de entrada
Living room	Sala de estar

www.LearnLikeNatives.com

PERGUNTAS

1) Por que Mary e Louise vão ao brechó?

    a) Elas precisam de dinheiro.

    b) Elas precisam de móveis, mas não têm muito dinheiro.

    c) Elas têm móveis para vender.

    d) Elas querem se divertir.

2) Por que os preços no brechó são tão baixos?

    a) É época de liquidação.

    b) O brechó está fechando.

    c) Os artigos são usados.

    d) Os preços são normais, não são baixos.

3) Qual dos seguintes itens fica na cozinha?

    a) cama

    b) micro-ondas

c) chuveiro

d) sofá

4) Como Nick sabe tanto sobre a pintura?

a) Ele é marchand profissional.

b) A pintura pertence a Nick.

c) Ele estuda arte.

d) Ele leu um livro.

5) No final, Mary e Louise estão....

a) tristes.

b) surpresas e ricas.

c) com raiva do Nick.

d) cansadas demais para fazer uma festa.

RESPOSTAS

1) Por que Mary e Louise vão ao brechó?

    b) Elas precisam de móveis, mas não têm muito dinheiro.

2) Por que os preços no brechó são tão baixos?

    c) Os itens são usados.

3) Qual dos seguintes itens fica na cozinha?

    b) micro-ondas

4) Como Nick sabe tanto sobre a pintura?

    c) Ele estuda arte.

5) No final, Mary e Louise estão...

    b) surpresas e ricas.

www.LearnLikeNatives.com

Translation of the Story

Thrift Store Bargain

STORY

Louise and Mary are best friends. They are also **roommates**. They share an **apartment** in the center of town. Today they want to shop for **furniture** for their **home**. Louise and Mary are both students. They do not have much money.

"Where can we shop?" Louise asks Mary.

"We need a lot of furniture," Mary says. She is worried about money.

"I know," says Louise. "We need to find a **bargain**."

"I have an idea. Let's go to the thrift store!" says Mary.

"Great idea!" says Louise.

The two girls drive the car to the thrift store. It is a giant store. The building is bigger than ten **houses**.

The girls park the car. The parking lot is empty.

"Wow," says Louise. "The store is very big."

"Totally," says Mary. "And there is nobody here."

www.LearnLikeNatives.com

"We will be the only people," says Louise. "We can **make ourselves at home.**"

The girls walk into the store. The store has everything. On the right, there is the **kitchen** section. There are tall **refrigerators** and old **microwaves** on the **shelves**. There are **toasters** of all colors. The prices are good. A microwave costs only $10.

Everything is a bargain. The items are used and second-hand. However, Mary and Louise find items that they like. There are more than a dozen sofas. Mary and Louise need a **sofa**. They spend time talking about the different sofas. Mary likes a brown leather sofa. Louise likes a big purple sofa. They cannot decide. Louise sees a purple **chair**. The girls decide to get the purple sofa and chair so that they match. It is perfect for their home.

"I need a **bed** for my **bedroom**," says Louise.

The girls walk to the bedroom area. First, they pass the art section.

"You know, we need something for the **walls**," says Louise. Mary agrees. There are big paintings, small paintings, empty **frames**, and photographs in frames. Louise decides on a big, abstract painting. It has lines of splattered red, blue, and black paint.

"I can paint like that," says Mary. "It looks like a child's painting."

"It's only five dollars," says Louise.

"Oh, ok!" says Mary.

The girls finish shopping. Louise also finds a **lamp** for her bedroom. Her bedroom is too dark. Mary chooses a **carpet** for the **bathroom**. The girls are very happy. They spend only $100 dollars for all the furniture.

"That is why shopping at the thrift store is a bargain," says Louise.

"Yes, we got **everything but the kitchen sink**!" says Mary.

Mary and Louise have a party in their apartment that night. It is a party to welcome friends. Mary and Louise want to show their new furniture.

The doorbell rings. Mary opens the **door**. Nick is the first to arrive. Nick is Mary's friend. Nick is also a student. He studies art history.

"Hi, ladies," says Nick. "Thank you for inviting me."

"Come in, Nick!" says Mary. Nick steps into the **foyer**. She hugs him.

"Do you want to see our new stuff?" asks Louise.

"Yeah!" says Nick.

Louise and Mary show Nick around the apartment. They are happy with the **living room**. The new sofa, chair and painting looks great.

"All of this is from the thrift store," says Mary. She is proud.

Nick walks up to the painting. "I really like this painting," he says.

"I do too," says Louise. "I chose it."

"It reminds me of Jackson Pollock," says Nick.

"Who is Jackson Pollock?" asks Mary.

"He is a very famous painter," says Nick. "He splashes paint onto canvas. Just like this one." Nick looks closely at the painting.

"Is it signed?" he asks. Louise shakes her head no. "Let's look behind it then."

They take the painting out of the frame and turn it around. They all are quiet. On the bottom is a signature that looks like 'Jackson Pollock'.

"How much did you pay for this?" asks Nick.

"About five dollars," says Louise.

"This is probably worth at least $10 million dollars," says Nick. He is shocked. Mary looks at Louise. Louise looks at Mary.

"Does anyone want a glass of champagne?" says Mary.

Now that is a bargain!

www.LearnLikeNatives.com

CHAPTER 3
The Goat / common present tense verbs

Ollie acorda. O sol está brilhando. Ele se lembra: é sábado. Hoje seu pai não **trabalha**. Isso significa que Ollie e o pai **fazem** algo juntos. O que eles podem fazer? Ollie **quer** ir ao cinema. Ele também quer jogar videogames.

Ollie tem doze anos. Ele **vai** à escola. No sábado, ele não vai à escola. Ele **usa** o sábado para fazer o que quer. O pai deixa Ollie decidir. Então Ollie quer fazer algo divertido.

— Paaai! — **chama** Ollie. — **Venha** aqui!

Ollie espera.

O pai entra no quarto de Ollie.

— Hoje é sábado — **diz** Ollie.

— Eu **sei**, filho — diz o pai do Ollie.

— Quero fazer algo divertido! — diz Ollie.

— Eu também — diz o pai.

— O que podemos fazer? — **pergunta** Ollie.

— O que você quer fazer?— pergunta o pai.

— Ir ao cinema — diz Ollie.

— Nós sempre vamos ao cinema no sábado — diz o pai do Ollie.

— Jogar videogames — diz Ollie.

— Jogamos videogames todos os dias! — diz o pai.

— Ok, ok — diz Ollie. Ele **pensa**. Ele se lembra de seu professor na escola. Seu professor **diz** aos alunos para saírem de casa. O professor ensina que o ar fresco é bom. Na escola, eles estudam os animais. Ollie aprende sobre animais da selva, animais do oceano e animais da fazenda.

É isso!

www.LearnLikeNatives.com

— Pai, vamos a uma fazenda! — diz Ollie. O pai do Ollie acha que é uma ótima ideia. Ele sempre quis **ver** e tocar os animais da fazenda.

Eles pegam o carro. O pai dirige para a zona rural. Eles veem uma placa que diz "Fazenda de Animais". Eles seguem as placas e estacionam o carro.

Ollie e o pai compram ingressos para entrar. Os ingressos custam $5. Eles deixam a bilheteria. Há um grande prédio de madeira, a casa da fazenda. Atrás da casa há um enorme campo. O campo tem árvores, grama e cercas. Em cada cerca há um tipo diferente de animal. Há centenas de animais.

Ollie está animado. Ele vê galinhas, cavalos, patos e porcos. Ele os toca e os escuta. Ollie **faz** um som para cada animal. Para os patos, ele diz "quack". Para os porcos, ele diz "óinc". Para os cavalos, ele diz "hinn". Para as galinhas, ele diz "cocó". Os animais olham fixamente para Ollie.

Depois dos animais em gaiolas, Ollie vê um rebanho de ovelhas. O pai lhe diz que as ovelhas são as fêmeas. Os machos são chamados carneiros. Os filhotes de ovelha são chamados cordeiros. As ovelhas estão comendo grama.

— Elas podem nos ver — diz o pai.

— Mas elas não estão olhando para nós — diz Ollie.

— As ovelhas podem ver o que está atrás delas. Elas não precisam virar a cabeça — diz o pai. O pai do Ollie sabe muito sobre ovelhas.

— Eles cortam o pelo das ovelhas na primavera — diz o pai. Ele diz ao Ollie que a lã das ovelhas **se**

transforma em suéteres, cachecóis e outras roupas quentes. Ollie tem um suéter feito de lã. Ele é quente.

Ollie e o pai andam pelo campo. A grama é verde. Há vacas em um canto. Uma das vacas alimenta um bezerro.

— Você sabe o que as vacas fazem, Ollie? — pergunta o pai.

— Dã! Leite! — diz Ollie.

— Isso mesmo — diz o pai.

Ollie ouve o som de um animal. Ele **pega** a mão do pai. Eles caminham na direção do som. Eles chegam a uma cerca. Eles **encontram** uma cabra. A cabra está com os chifres presos na cerca.

A cabra está sentada no chão. Ela não se move. Seus chifres estão entre as tábuas e ela não pode se mover. Ollie e o pai **olham** para a cabra.

— Estou com muita pena da cabra — diz Ollie. Ela parece triste.

— Coitada! — diz o pai.

— Ela parece tão triste — diz Ollie.

— Podemos ajudá-la — diz o pai.

— Sim! — diz Ollie.

Eles se aproximam da cabra. Ollie está nervoso. O pai diz para ele não se preocupar. Os chifres estão presos e a cabra não vai machucá-los. Ollie olha nos olhos da cabra. A cabra **precisa** de ajuda. Ollie fala com a cabra. Ele **tenta** fazer sons suaves. Ele quer manter a cabra calma.

O pai do Ollie tenta mover os chifres. Ele tenta o chifre direito. Ele tenta o chifre esquerdo. Eles não se movem. Depois de dez minutos, eles **desistem**.

— Não consigo — diz o pai do Ollie.

— Você tem certeza? — pergunta Ollie.

— Os chifres estão presos — diz o pai.

— O que fazemos? — pergunta Ollie.

A área ao redor da cabra é lama. Não há mais grama. O pai do Ollie pega um pouco de grama do chão e a traz para a cabra. A cabra come a grama. A cabra parece faminta. A grama acaba. Ollie pega mais grama para dar para a cabra. Eles fazem carinho na cabra por alguns minutos. A cabra parece agradecida.

— Vamos avisar o dono — diz o pai.

— Sim — diz Ollie. — Talvez eles possam ajudá-la.

Ollie e o pai vão para a bilheteria. A bilheteria é um pequeno prédio na entrada. Um homem trabalha lá. Ollie e o pai entram.

— Olá, senhor — diz o pai do Ollie.

— Como posso ajudá-los? — pergunta o homem.

— Há uma cabra... — diz o pai do Ollie.

O homem interrompe o pai do Ollie. Ele acena com a mão. Ele parece entediado. — Sim, nós sabemos.

— Você sabe sobre a cabra? — pergunta Ollie.

— A cabra presa na cerca? — pergunta o homem.

— Sim! — dizem Ollie e o pai.

— Ah sim, é a Patty — diz o homem. — Ela pode se soltar quando quiser. Ela só gosta de atenção.

Ollie **dá** um olhar surpreso ao pai. Ollie e o pai riem.

— Patty, que cabra! — diz Ollie.

RESUMO

Ollie acorda no sábado. Ele e seu pai decidem fazer algo divertido. Eles vão para uma fazenda para ver animais. Eles veem e tocam muitos animais: vacas, cavalos, ovelhas e muito mais. Eles andam pela fazenda. É um belo dia. Eles encontram uma cabra presa em uma cerca. Eles tentam ajudar a cabra. A cabra está presa pelos chifres. Eles lhe dão grama. Ollie e o pai vão **buscar** ajuda. O homem da bilheteria os escuta. Ele diz que a cabra gosta de enganar as pessoas para ganhar atenção. Ollie e o pai riem.

LISTA DE VOCABULÁRIO

To work	Trabalhar
To do	Fazer
To want	Querer
To go	Ir
To use	Usar
To call	Chamar
To come	Vir
To say	Dizer
To know	Saber
To ask	Perguntar
To think	Pensar

www.LearnLikeNatives.com

To tell	Dizer
To see	Ver
To become	Se transformar
To make	Fazer
To take	Pegar
To find	Encontrar
To feel	Sentir
To look	Olhar
To get	Buscar
To need	Precisar
To try	Tentar
To give	Dar

www.LearnLikeNatives.com

PERGUNTAS

1) O que Ollie e o pai decidem fazer no sábado?

    a) ir ao cinema

    b) Ir a uma fazenda

    c) jogar videogames

    d) ir à escola

2) Sobre que animal o pai do Ollie sabe muito?

    a) ovelha

    b) porco

    c) girafa

    d) vaca

3) O que está acontecendo com a cabra?

    a) ela está escondida

b) ela está comendo

c) ela está presa

d) ela está com raiva

4) O que Ollie e o pai fazem pela cabra?

    a) soltam

    b) dão grama e fazem carinho

    c) chamam a polícia para buscá-la

    d) beijam

5) O que a Patty faz?

    a) Deixa a fazenda

    b) ela come lixo

    c) vai para a bilheteira

    d) finge que está presa para chamar atenção

www.LearnLikeNatives.com

RESPOSTAS

1) O que Ollie e o pai decidem fazer no sábado?

    b) Ir a uma fazenda

2) Sobre que animal o pai do Ollie sabe muito?

    a) ovelha

3) O que está acontecendo com a cabra?

    c) ela está presa

4) O que Ollie e o pai fazem pela cabra?

    b) dão grama e fazem carinho

5) O que a Patty faz?

    d) finge que está presa para chamar atenção

www.LearnLikeNatives.com

Translation of the Story

The Goat

Ollie wakes up. The sun is shining. He remembers: it is Saturday. Today his dad does not **work**. That means Ollie and his dad **do** something together. What can they do? Ollie **wants** to go to the movies. He also wants to play video games.

Ollie is twelve years old. He goes to school. Saturday he does not go to school. He **uses** Saturday to do what he wants. His dad lets him decide. So Ollie wants to do something fun.

"Daaaaaad!" **calls** Ollie. "**Come** here!"

Ollie waits.

His dad enters Ollie's bedroom.

"Today is Saturday," **says** Ollie.

"I **know**, son," says Ollie's dad.

"I want to do something fun!" says Ollie.

"Me too," says Dad.

"What can we do?" **asks** Ollie.

"What do you want to do?" asks his dad.

"Go to the movies," says Ollie.

"We always go to the movies on Saturday," says Ollie's dad.

"Play video games," says Ollie.

"We play video games everyday!" says Dad.

"Ok, ok," says Ollie. He **thinks**. He remembers his teacher at school. His teacher **tells** the students to go outside. The teacher tells them the fresh air is good. At school, they study animals. Ollie learns about animals in the jungle, animals in the ocean, and animals on farms.

That's it!

"Dad, let's go to a farm!" says Ollie. Ollie's dad thinks that is a great idea. He has always wanted to **see** and touch farm animals.

They take the car. Ollie's dad drives to the countryside. They see a sign that says "Animal Farm". They follow the signs and park the car.

Ollie and his dad buy tickets to enter. Tickets cost $5. They leave the ticket office. There is a big wooden building, the farmhouse. Behind the farmhouse, there is a huge field. The field has trees, grass, and fences. In each fence is a different type of animal. There are hundreds of animals.

Ollie is excited. He sees chickens, horses, ducks, and pigs. He touches them and listens to them. Ollie **makes** a sound to each animal. To the ducks, he says "quack". To the pigs, he says "oink". To the horses, he says "nay". To the chickens, he says "bok bok". The animals stare at Ollie.

Past the animals in cages, Ollie sees a flock of sheep. Ollie's dad tells him that female sheep are called ewes. Male sheep are rams. Baby sheep are called lambs. The sheep are eating grass.

"They can see us," says Dad.

"But they are not looking at us," says Ollie.

"Sheep can see behind themselves. They don't have to turn their heads," says Dad. Ollie's dad knows a lot about sheep.

"They cut the hair on the sheep in spring," says Dad. He tells Ollie how the sheep's wool **becomes** sweaters, scarves and other warm clothing. Ollie has a sweater made of wool. It is warm.

Ollie and his dad walk around the field. The grass is green. There are cows in a corner. One of the mother cows feeds a baby calf.

"You know what cows make, Ollie?" asks Dad.

"Duh! Milk!" says Ollie.

"That's right," says Dad.

Ollie hears an animal sound. He **takes** his dad's hand. They walk towards the sound. They come to a fence. They **find** a goat. The goat has horns stuck in the fence. The goat sits on the ground. It does not move. Its horns are between the wood and it can't move. Ollie and his dad **look** at the goat.

"I feel so bad for the goat," says Ollie. She seems sad.

"Poor guy!" says Dad.

"He looks so sad," says Ollie.

"We can help him," Dad says.

"Yeah!" says Ollie.

They get close to the goat. Ollie is nervous. Dad says not to worry. The horns are stuck and the goat will not hurt them. Ollie looks into the eyes of the goat. The goat **needs** help. Ollie talks to the goat. He **tries** to make soft sounds. He wants to keep the goat calm.

Ollie's dad tries to move the horns. He tries the right horn. He tries the left horn. They don't move. After ten minutes, they **give up**.

"I can't do it," says Ollie's dad.

"Are you sure?" asks Ollie.

"The horns are stuck," says Dad.

"What do we do?" asks Ollie.

The area around the goat is mud. There is no grass left. Ollie's dad takes some grass from the ground and brings it to the goat. The goat eats the grass. The goat looks hungry. The grass is gone. Ollie gets more grass to take to the goat. They pet the goat for a few minutes. The goat seems grateful.

"Let's tell the owner," says Dad.

"Yeah," says Ollie. "Maybe they can help her."

Ollie and his dad go to the ticket office. The ticket office is a small building at the entrance. A man works there. Ollie and his dad go inside.

"Hello, sir," says Ollie's dad.

"How can I help you?" asks the man.

"There's a goat—" says Ollie's dad.

The man interrupts Ollie's dad. He waves his hand. He looks bored. "Yeah, we know."

"You know about the goat?" asks Ollie.

"The goat stuck in the fence?" asks the man.

"Yes!" say Ollie and his dad.

"Oh yes, that's Patty," says the man. "She can get herself out whenever she wants. She just likes the attention."

Ollie **gives** his dad a surprised look. Ollie and his dad laugh.

"Patty, what a goat!" Ollie says.

www.LearnLikeNatives.com

CONCLUSION

You did it!

You finished a whole book in a brand new language. That in and of itself is quite the accomplishment, isn't it?

Congratulate yourself on time well spent and a job well done. Now that you've finished the book, you have familiarized yourself with over 500 new vocabulary words, comprehended the heart of 3 short stories, and listened to loads of dialogue unfold, all without going anywhere!

Charlemagne said "To have another language is to possess a second soul." After immersing yourself in this book, you are broadening your horizons and opening a whole new path for yourself.

Have you thought about how much you know now that you did not know before? You've learned everything from how to greet and how to express your emotions to basics like colors and place words. You can tell time and ask question. All without opening a schoolbook. Instead, you've cruised through fun, interesting stories and possibly listened to them as well.

Perhaps before you weren't able to distinguish meaning when you listened to Brazilian Portuguese. If you used the audiobook, we bet you can now pick out meanings and words when you hear someone speaking. Regardless, we are sure you have taken an important step to being more fluent. You are well on your way!

Best of all, you have made the essential step of distinguishing in your mind the idea that most often hinders people studying a new language. By approaching Brazilian Portuguese through our short stories and dialogs, instead of formal lessons with just grammar and vocabulary, you are no longer in the 'learning' mindset. Your approach is much more similar to an osmosis, focused on speaking and using the language, which is the end goal, after all!

So, what's next?

This is just the first of five books, all packed full of short stories and dialogs, covering essential, everyday Brazilian Portuguese that will ensure you master the basics. You can find the rest of the books in the series, as well as a whole host of other resources, at LearnLikeNatives.com. Simply add the book to your library to take the next step in your language learning journey. If you are ever in need of new ideas or direction, refer to our 'Speak Like a Native' eBook, available to you for free at LearnLikeNatives.com, which clearly outlines practical steps you can take to continue learning any language you choose.

We also encourage you to get out into the real world and practice your Brazilian Portuguese. You have a leg up on most beginners, after all—instead of pure textbook learning, you have been absorbing the sound and soul of the language. Do not underestimate the foundation you have built reviewing the chapters of this book. Remember, no one feels 100% confident when they speak with a native speaker in another language.

One of the coolest things about being human is connecting with others. Communicating with someone in their own language is a wonderful gift. Knowing the language turns you into a local and opens up your world. You will see the reward of learning languages for many years to come, so keep that practice up!. Don't let your fears stop you from taking the chance to use your Brazilian Portuguese. Just give it a try, and remember that you will make mistakes. However, these mistakes will teach you so much, so view every single one as a small victory! Learning is growth.

Don't let the quest for learning end here! There is so much you can do to continue the learning process in an organic way, like you did with this book. Add another book from Learn Like a Native to your library. Listen to Brazilian Portuguese talk radio. Watch some of the great Brazilian Movies. Put on the latest CD from Tom Jobim. Take Samba lessons in Portuguese. Whatever you do, don't stop because every little step you take counts towards learning a new language, culture, and way of communicating.

www.LearnLikeNatives.com

www.LearnLikeNatives.com

www.LearnLikeNatives.com

Learn Like a Native is a revolutionary **language education brand** that is taking the linguistic world by storm. Forget boring grammar books that never get you anywhere, Learn Like a Native teaches you languages in a fast and fun way that actually works!

As an international, multichannel, language learning platform, we provide **books, audio guides and eBooks** so that you can acquire the knowledge you need, swiftly and easily.

Our **subject-based learning**, structured around real-world scenarios, builds your conversational muscle and ensures you learn the content most relevant to your requirements. Discover our tools at ***LearnLikeNatives.com***.

When it comes to learning languages, we've got you covered!

www.ingramcontent.com/pod-product-compliance
Lightning Source LLC
Chambersburg PA
CBHW070042230426
43661CB00005B/720